WE
THE PEOPLE
CRAZY HORSE

Published by Creative Education, Inc. 123 South
Broad Street, Mankato, Minnesota 56001

Library of Congress Cataloging-in-Publication Data

Rothaus, James.
  Crazy Horse.

  (We the people)
  Summary: A biography of the Oglala chief who relent-
lessly resisted the white man's attempts to take over
Indian lands.
  1. Crazy Horse, ca. 1842-1877-Juvenile literature.
2. Oglala Indians—Biography—Juvenile literature.
3. Dakota Indians—Wars—Juvenile literature.   4. Indians
of North America—Great Plains—Wars—Juvenile literature.
[1. Crazy Horse, ca. 1842-1877.   2. Oglala Indians—
Biography.   3. Indians of North America—Biography]
I. Title.   II. Series: We the people (Mankato, Minn.)
E99.O3C727   1987   978.00497 [B] [92]   87-27144
ISBN 0-88682-163-0

WE
THE PEOPLE
CRAZY HORSE

WAR CHIEF OF THE OGLALA
(1841-1887)

JAMES R. ROTHAUS

Illustrated By John Keely And Dick Brude

CREATIVE EDUCATION

CRAZY HORSE

Long before the white settlers came to their lands, the Plains Indians were respected as the great hunters and warriors of the prairies. They could ride like the wind on horseback.

By day, they hunted the buffalo or battled with other tribes to protect their hunting grounds. At night, their council fires glowed across the lands we now know as Iowa, Kansas, Wyoming, Missouri, Nebraska, Montana, and into the Dakotas.

Of all the Plains Indians, the most fierce and most numerous were the Lakota. White men called them the Sioux. There were seven tribes in the Sioux nation. One of the largest was the Oglala.

The Oglala were proud hunters who loved to roam and be free. They respected the land, the water, the wind, the sky, the animals and each other. Though they hunted the buffalo for food and clothing, the Oglala honored the herds in art and song, thanking the buffalo for giving them life.

About 1841, a son was born to Crazy Horse, a spiritual leader of the Oglala. The boy had fine brown hair and they called him Curly. When he was still very small, Curly decided to become a warrior.

A warrior named Hump became Curly's "older brother," teaching him to hunt and fight. When

Curly was ten, Hump took him to the great council at Fort Laramie. There the white soldiers said that the Indians would be given presents if they kept the peace. The Indians were not to molest white travelers on the Medicine Road—the Oregon Trail.

Curly watched and listened. He wondered why the soldiers insisted that the Indians sign a piece of paper called a treaty. He thought the soldiers should do as the Indians do. He thought they should speak slowly and clearly from their hearts, and then live by their words. An Indian's promise needed no piece of paper to back it up.

Two years went by. More and more white settlers were moving

westward along the Medicine Road through Indian country. The Oglala were saddened by the deep cuts made by the settlers' wagon wheels in the earth. But they lived by their promise to keep peace.

Then one day there was trouble. In 1854, when Curly was about 13, a white settler said that an Indian stole his cow. Chief Con-

quering Bear tried to tell a white army officer that it was all a mistake.

The officer misunderstood. He told his troops to fire on the Indians. The chief fell dead and the angry Indians killed all the soldiers.

From that day on, young Curly grew fearful and bitter towards white men.

It was a custom among the Oglala for a young man to go alone into the wilderness and pray. This custom was called a "Vision Quest."

When Curly was 14, he went on his Vision Quest. He asked God to give him a dream of power. The boy dreamed of a storm and a hawk. His father said this meant he would lead his people in battle.

Hump took Curly into his first battle a few years later. The boy fought bravely against the Grass House Indians. The tribe proclaimed him a man. And Curly felt honored to receive his father's name, Crazy Horse.

Years passed. Crazy Horse became a great warrior. His battles were mostly with other Indian tribes.

But he often heard about Indians and whites fighting to the south.

One day, an Indian messenger brought bad news. White soldiers had attacked a peaceful village, killing 100 families. Crazy Horse felt the fear and anger rise up inside his heart again. The promises made in the white treaty were empty. Hump, Crazy Horse, and many other Oglalas joined a group of Sioux who declared war on the whites.

The Sioux Wars began about 1865. For three years the Indians fought the U.S. Army. Crazy Horse became a war leader of one large group. Chief Sitting Bull led another.

In 1868, the U.S. Government tried to make peace by giving

the Indians a huge reservation. "All this land shall be yours," the white men said, "as long as the grass shall grow and the water flow."

Some Indians believed it. They were weary of fighting, and they yearned for peace. But Crazy Horse and Sitting Bull had seen too many white promises broken before. Their people kept on fighting. They had only scorn for the reservation Indians. How could white men give them land that was already theirs? How could Indian people live in peace, when all around them were armed men whose words could not be trusted?

Several years went by. Crazy Horse vowed he would never live on the reservation with the other

Indians. He was chief of a large band
of Oglalas who felt the same way.
They roamed the open prairies,

hunting and fighting as their ancestors had done for thousands of years.

Stories about Chief Crazy Horse and his renegade warriors were told again and again across the country. As the legend of Crazy Horse grew, the U.S. cavalry officers felt embarrassed. This worried the reservation Indians. If the soldiers hated Crazy Horse, would they start to hate the reservation Indians, too?

Then something happened that united many of the reservation Indians with Crazy Horse and his renegades.

In 1875, the U.S. Government tried to force the Sioux to sell part of their big reservation—the holy Black Hills country. This was

the same land that was promised to the red men "as long as the grass shall grow." So much for white promises!

Crazy Horse and his people joined Sitting Bull and other Indian leaders for a last stand against the white army. About 1,000 Indians, led by Crazy Horse and Sitting Bull, fought General Crook's men at Rosebud Creek, June 17, 1876. The Indians won.

General Crook retreated and called for more men. The Indians moved their camp to the Little Big Horn River and waited.

A week later, an army officer named George Armstrong Custer disobeyed orders and attacked the Indian camp with a force of less than

700 men. General Custer was a vain man. He thought he would become famous by killing the great chief, Crazy Horse.

Instead, the ones who died were Custer and more than 200 of his men. Crazy Horse led 3,000 Indians to the attack that day. They fought for the sacred land where their forefathers were buried. They fought for their way of life, for the buffalo, and for the future of their families. In the years to come, the history books would call this famous fight The Battle of Little Big Horn, or "Custer's Last Stand." But, it was actually the last stand for the Indians. No wonder they fought so fiercely!

Crazy Horse killed many but

he himself was not wounded. After the battle, he and the other Indian leaders met with Sitting Bull, who was leader of all the Sioux. There

was no time to celebrate their victory over the soldiers. Another white army was coming, and this one was sure to be even bigger than the last.

Sitting Bull wanted the Indians to gather their families and flee to safety in Canada. But it was such a long journey. Many of the people did not want to leave the country they had fought so hard to protect. Finally, a council was held, and decisions were made.

Crazy Horse would lead one large group and Sitting Bull another. Sitting Bull would go north while Crazy Horse would go south and then east, back to the sacred Black Hills. He and his young men would take up their war against the settlers again.

The moment came when Sitting Bull and Crazy Horse bade each other farewell. There was courage in their eyes, but sadness in their hearts.

A large white army under General Nelson A. Miles pursued the Indians. Many were captured and sent to the reservation. But Crazy Horse and his people still fought through the summer and fall.

Then came the winter, one of the worst the Indians had known. The north wind howled down across the plains, hurling huge mounds of snow and ice against the Indian teepees. Buffalo were scarce and the people became hungry, weak and discouraged. In January 1877, General Miles attacked Crazy Horse's camp. The people fled.

The Indians had no more bul-

lets or gunpowder. Their great victory on the Little Big Horn had been a glorious one, but there were too many white men. For every white soldier that fell, five would come to replace him.

Starving and freezing, the Oglalas were chased over the frozen plains. Often the white men sent

them messages. "Give up. Come into the reservation."

The people were losing heart. And Crazy Horse's own wife, Black Shawl, was sick with the coughing disease.

Old Indian friends came to Crazy Horse and begged him to give up. Crazy Horse listened silently to their words, and then he searched his own heart. He asked God for the courage and wisdom to be a good chief—to make the right decision. At last Crazy Horse agreed. It was the only way the proud chief could save his people from death.

On May 6, 1877, Crazy Horse surrendered at Fort Robinson, Nebraska. He brought about 1,000 of his people into the Red Cloud

Agency. The white leaders promised Crazy Horse an agency of his own. They said he would be allowed to go to Washington and talk to the Great Father about his people.

But this promise was not kept.

Some of the Sioux on the reservation made trouble for Crazy Horse.

Indians who were jealous told the whites that Crazy Horse was going to lead a revolt. On September 4, 1877, when the chief brought his sick wife to visit her family, he was arrested.

Red men who hated him grabbed his arms. White soldiers who thought he was escaping, stabbed him. He died the next day. His sorrowing people hid his body where whites would never find it.

Crazy Horse, the great chief who had fought so bravely to protect the Indian people and their land, was gone. But even today his courage and struggle lives on in the hearts of Native Americans.

WE THE PEOPLE SERIES

WOMEN OF AMERICA

CLARA BARTON
JANE ADDAMS
ELIZABETH BLACKWELL
HARRIET TUBMAN
SUSAN B. ANTHONY
DOLLEY MADISON

INDIANS OF AMERICA

GERONIMO
CRAZY HORSE
CHIEF JOSEPH
PONTIAC
SQUANTO
OSCEOLA

FRONTIERSMEN OF AMERICA

DANIEL BOONE
BUFFALO BILL
JIM BRIDGER
FRANCIS MARION
DAVY CROCKETT
KIT CARSON

WAR HEROES OF AMERICA

JOHN PAUL JONES
PAUL REVERE
ROBERT E. LEE
ULYSSES S. GRANT
SAM HOUSTON
LAFAYETTE

EXPLORERS OF AMERICA

COLUMBUS
LEIF ERICSON
DeSOTO
LEWIS AND CLARK
CHAMPLAIN
CORONADO